NETWORKING

Learn How to Influence Others and Boost Your Social Skills. Career Growth, Jobs, Social Skills & Approach

within this book without the consent of the author or copyright owner. Legal action will be pursued if this is breached.

Disclaimer Notice:

Please note the information contained within this document is for educational and entertainment purposes only. Every attempt has been made to provide accurate, up to date and reliable complete information. No warranties of any kind are expressed or implied. Readers acknowledge that the author is not engaging in the rendering of legal, financial, medical or professional advice.

Table of Contents

Introduction

Networking provides us with an invaluable tool with which to promote both ourselves and our companies. Whether you are trying to sell a product, a service or line yourself up for a new job this is the one skill you must have to forward your goals. Why do you think it is that eighty percent on top executive positions are filled without being advertised?

I think that most of us are aware, at least to a certain degree, how important it is to network in the modern-day business environment and yet this remains one of the most underutilized weapons in our armory. Why? Because for many of us, engaging with strangers is difficult and uncomfortable. We would far rather sit in the security of our office banging out copy for brochures and press releases than actually take the bold step of going face to face with someone we have never met before. This despite the fact that deep down, we realize how many doors could be opened if we were just a little bolder.

Well here is something to take into consideration: very few people are confident in engaging with strangers, they have just learned the importance of stepping outside of their comfort zones. Sure some people are naturally so gregarious that they could approach a barn door and enter into conversation but for most of the others, getting out there and mixing demands a set of skills they have had to learn and develop. If others can foster these valuable skills then so can you and perhaps it's high time you did.

At their core, networking skills are interpersonal skills and that means that they extend beyond our work environment. Although we will look at most of the techniques we cover in this book from a business stand point, these methods translate into every walk of life where we interact with people. Understanding the needs of others and communicating those needs of our own in a way that makes them readily acceptable is more than just networking, it is an essential life skill.

Chapter 1: Getting Down to Basics

Where to network

In an age of technology and with an arsenal of social media resources like LinkedIn, Facebook and WhatsApp at our fingertips it might seem that the need for face to face networking has diminished, if not died altogether. Many of you, I am sure, are taking a great big sigh and thinking what a relief that is. What the experts will tell you, however, is that the need for interpersonal relationships are greater than they ever were and though these social media tools are useful accessories they simply lack the depth to create an initial connection with any substance to it.

The fact is we still need to get out there and make contacts and open the doors to communication. Just thinking of this probably gives you a knot in your stomach and even as you read this your mind is looking for ways to sidestep any such discomfort. Well here are two small items of good news: One, everyone else out there is as uncomfortable as you are and two, once you start to practice the skills set out in this book things will begin to get easier. I don't promise you it will ever be a walk in the park but with a little effort, one day you might be able to step confidently into a room of total strangers and make it look like it is.

Our network is all around us if we start to look. Obviously though, there are some environments that are more strategically advantageous to us than others and these are going to vary according to our specific business or career situations. Make sure to target the ones that will put you with the right people rather than those that will put you with people that are easier to talk to who but who offer little or no hope of advancing your cause. I say this because when venturing out of our comfort zones it is easy to choose the path of least resistance and then kid ourselves that because we are doing something we must be moving forward. If you are promoting the latest high tech computer software do not get into an hour long talk about it with the petrol attendant in the hope that he will run into somebody with a need for your product.

Many larger companies host charity events and fundraisers for various causes. These are great opportunities to meet people with similar business interests and needs to your own. Though these may have the appearance of social gatherings, when you scrape away the thin outer veneer, they are often networking events. The people organizing these sorts of functions are often desperate for reliable people to lengthen their guest lists for future events. Make sure you let it be known that you are interested and you can be sure you will start to receive regular invites. While you are about it, chat to the organizer and find out a little about them; it is most likely that they have a network that is quite impressive and if you let them know a little about yourself, you are suddenly networking already.

Sporting events and clubs are another area where plenty of business gets done and contacts get made. The beauty about networking and sport is that you immediately have an area of common interest and a relaxed atmosphere. They say that there is more business done on the golf course than there ever is round the board room table. If like me you have the capacity to aim a golf ball in one direction and then hit it in a different, and often surprising, direction altogether there are plenty of other sports out there. I ran for a social running club that was more about socializing than running but the contacts that I developed out of that were incredibly useful to my business.

For some people, sports events may simply be beyond the pale and the company might not be connected to any fund raising organizations. Well these are just two examples that spring to mind but there are plenty of others out there if you decide to look. Beyond that there are organizations that stage networking events and that takes any of the initial effort off of your hands. On the internet there are groups like Get Konnected but there are also companies that stage networking events that may be targeted to your specific product or profession and they will be more than happy to add your name to their next function list, though you might have to pay.

Chapter 2: Getting the Ball Rolling

OK So now you have chosen the event at which you are going to start your networking debut. You are now getting nervous, your palms are starting to sweat and you are desperately trying to conjure up a fever so you can shy off and not go.

Research

Instead of listening to your fears concentrate on doing something positive. Start by researching who is going to be there. If you are going to an organized function ask the organizer for a guest list in advance and don't by ashamed to ask the organizer who she recommends you try to talk to. Once you have targeted a few likely people with whom it would be good to make contact then hit the internet and find out as much about them and their companies as you can. Ask around and see if you can glean any advance information from your colleagues. What you are trying to do here is not spy on the person. You are looking for conversation handles and common ground that might make it easier to get them talking.

If your research does not throw up any information about the people you hope to network with then make sure you are up to date with a broad range of current events. What is going on in the world of sport, politics and within your industry are all conversation toeholds that will be useful to have. In many instances the first few minutes after an introduction awkward. If you have a few, easy to use, small conversation feeders, then you can take the tension out of that initial situation. What is more the very fact that you have relaxed the atmosphere will mean that you begin to be perceived as influential in the eyes of others.

Breaking the ice

For all of us this is probably the hardest part of any social interaction be it a networking event or a social gathering of some kind. If you step into a room filled with total strangers your natural instincts are defensive and you tend to make for the most out of the way corner from which you can observe whilst remaining as invisible as possible. In essence you are retreating to a cave.

Be aware that this is likely to be your first reaction and instead place yourself in a position where you can observe but where you are not hiding. This serves two purposes. It exposes you to others who may be in a similar position to yourself and may therefore approach you whilst at the same time allows you to look around and see who is the most approachable.

Studies reveal that people decide whether they like you or not within the first seven seconds of meeting you. This means that whether you decide to approach someone or are approached by somebody else you need to present a good impression. The impression you want to deliver is one of open approachability. Start off with a smile. Smiling is incredibly important at breaking down barriers. It says I am friendly and mean no harm. Whether someone approaches you or you approach first, offer a firm (not knuckle breaking handshake) and introduce yourself. Follow that up with some light conversation starters designed to elicit conversation. To do this ask an open ended question that requires a response of greater depth than a simple yes or no. Hopefully the person with whom you are talking will now begin to open up. If not have one or two follow up questions that are light and easy to turn into conversation.

Now the conversation has started, you have broken the ice and your next task is to be interesting. To be interesting is easy. We are all the most interesting people we know so if you can get the person with whom you are conversing to talk about themselves you will appear interesting without having given much more than your name. Listen attentively. This demands that we become active listeners and being an active listener is an invaluable skill to have. People like to talk about themselves but they need to be made to feel that what they have to say is of interest (even if it isn't). Maintain eye contact. There is nothing worse than talking to someone who is constantly glancing away to see who else in the room may be a better contact. For the moment whoever you are talking to is the most important person in the room. Nod in agreement from time to time and ask questions that will demonstrate that you are paying attention. Already you are smiling, relaxed and engaged in conversation and giving the appearance of being in control. You are starting to become a person that others are drawn to.

Let's not forget that your primary reason for putting yourself through this torturous event is to grow your network. Listen to the person with whom you have already engaged and make a mental note of any information that may be useful in continuing the conversation at a later date. Look for areas of commonality. These could be business interests, leisure activities or just having kids of the same sort of age. It doesn't matter. You are just mentally filing this for use at a later date. If you realize that there is no networking advantage to be gained through continuing this conversation then wait for an appropriate moment to make your excuses and politely slip away. The other person may offer no business development possibilities for you but their own fear of finding themselves alone in the room could mean that they are clinging to you just so they don't have to go it alone. You don't want to hurt any feelings here so at the right moment make your excuses and move onto another group or person to connect with.

Expanding the circle

Whether or not we make a useful contact on our first attempt it is a good idea to circulate and meet as many people as possible if your network is to grow. The procedures are the same with each now person you encounter but I would hope by now you have begun to develop a bit more confidence and further introductions are easier. By now you should have at least given the appearance of being relaxed and in control and you need to live up to your own image. In each new encounter ask questions, listen actively and look for areas of commonality. You will start to meet people with whom you know you can do further business. Continue to ask about themselves but throw in the odd bit of information about yourself and your own business or personal interests. Don't give away too much but offer enough tid bits that they can follow up on if they in return are interested. If they do start to take an interest in who you or your company are then be sure that you have definite and concise information that you can give quickly and easily. Don't go into a long monologue, just be precise and positive. This is the start up meeting aimed at opening doors. It is not the time to try to sell yourself hard or close a sale. A big word of warning here: Just as everyone else loves to talk about themselves so too do we. Talking about our own lives, goals and interests may be the most interesting thing we can do but it is not always quite as interesting to others. Don't fall into the trap of hogging the limelight. You may wake up the next day thinking what an interesting evening you had and then realize that you talked about nothing but yourself and learnt nothing about anyone else. Always keep in mind the primary goal is to expand your network.

Chapter 3: Conversation; The Delicate Art

We have touched on the early stages of conversation, the use of questions and breaking the ice but where do we go from there. At the heart of every relationship there lies a large element of conversation and networking is a somewhat of a business term for relationship. We have already touched on this subject in terms of listening skills and question asking but it is of such importance to what we are trying to do that I think it is important to dig deeper into what makes a good conversationalist. You cannot be a good networker if you don't have good conversational skills. It is that simple.

As we have already seen there are some pitfalls in the arena of conversation. One is our own to desire to talk about ourselves and voice our own opinions. We all have a natural desire to have our voices heard and if we want to network we do need to make some statements about who we are and what we are about. It is that delicate balancing act of getting information across whilst remaining interested in others that we need to look at closely here.

Whether we are relating one on one or participating in a group conversation there are certain rules we should try to follow. A good starting point is how you position yourself. When dealing one on one face the other person as squarely as possible and keep you body language open and relaxed. This makes it easier to be seen to listen actively and also to put in your own concise and thought out statements when the opportunity presents itself. In a group try to position yourself so that you are not pushed to the outer extremes from where you are less likely to be noticed and will have more difficulty being heard.

Once the conversation gets going I like to take on the role of active observer. In groups this can be particularly advantageous because group conversation is a bit of a battlefield with everyone anxious to jump in and have their say. By observing you will get a feel for who those are who genuinely have something important to offer and those who just like to make the most noise. Often they are not the same people. Also it may be that the person or people you need to network with the most are not the ones doing the talking. Once you have established who is who in the group then decide when would be an appropriate time to enter the conversation and bear in mind your talk time is going to be limited so be careful choose your words carefully. Don't forget to listen out for conversation handles at a later date when people you would like to network with are speaking.

In a group conversation you will often find one or two people on the peripheries who would like to say something but are drowned out or dominated by those more able to push themselves forward. Here is your chance to do something for the underdog that may pay off in the future. Invite them into the conversation and don't be afraid to do so quite overtly but cutting someone off and saying words to the effect that "I think that so and so has something to add to that". This little act of kindness demonstrates compassion on your part and that person will possibly be grateful enough to try to garner your opinion later. You never know. You may just be triggering a network opportunity without realizing it.

In group conversations, especially when they are in quite formal surroundings where not all the players are familiar with one another there can be sudden breaks in the conversation where everything goes deathly quiet and it all becomes a little stiff and embarrassing. Be prepared for this and have a question at your finger tips so that you can be seen to be the one who takes control and averts and awkward moment.

Your research and general knowledge will come into play now and you should have a number of light but interesting subjects that you can bring into use to keep conversation going. This very gentle oiling of the conversation along with your capacity to ask questions that lead to further conversation will subtly give you a position of control in these engagements and appearing to be in control makes you a more attractive person to network with.

Beware of those subjects that are controversial. You and the other members of the group will undoubtedly have subjects that you feel passionate about. Whilst passionate conversation and debate can make for a stimulating and enjoyable evening that is not what you are looking for on this occasion. Your job is to establish contacts and in this day and age where there is always somebody who is desperate to be offended about something controversy is not what you seek. In subjects that one is passionate about it is all too easy to lose control and give voice to your opinions and then drive yourself into defending them. In any other environment that would be fine but not in this one.

On the other hand, if one of the other members of the group is foolish enough to voice a radical opinion it is a fine time to continue your subtle observations and see where the rest of the group stand and find who is passionate about what. It is all vital information to file away for a later date.

The same goes for humor. I recommend having some mild clean humor on standby. It can be an excellent tool for developing rapport. Bear in mind that there is usually someone who is the brunt of any joke. Once again you will need to be careful and err on the side of the politically correct. In general government and big institutions are widely acceptable targets but my favorite is to make jokes of which I am the fall guy. This way I am sure I won't cause any offence. By the same instance don't let anyone in the group start making fun of someone unable to defend themselves. There is no need to be rude but just try to steer the conversation in a different direction. Nobody likes a bully and though they might not have the courage to stand up to one, they will appreciate the fact that you do.

Chapter 4: The Follow Up

I really hope that by using these basic listening and questioning techniques you have not only developed your conversational skills but that you have begun to feel more comfortable with these situations that are so often awkward to start with. The good news is that the worst is over and whilst there is still much to be done, none of it will be as painful as that ice breaking first meeting. In large convention type scenarios things will start to settle down as the cocktails begin to flow and everyone has had a bit to of time to get to know one another and drop those masks they first entered the room with. Even in one on one meetings things should have moved on from small talk to things a little more pertinent to where you want them to be.

Continue with your gentle questions, always looking for handles but don't forget that these are mainly for use at a later date. Don't allow your questions to take on the appearance of an interrogation. Instead let them demonstrate that you are interested in the person or the people with who you are conversing. Now is the time to carefully start introducing a little information about yourself, your product or whatever else it is you are eventually hoping to promote. You are not trying to actually do any real promoting, just lay the ground work for a meeting at a later stage. Because you have listened so attentively to the other person you have created a situation in which they will hopefully feel obliged to listen to you. This is known as reciprocity and it is an incredibly valuable networking tool that we shall visit again later in this book.

Having created some opening through which to set up further meetings it is time to start to think about moving on. You need to cast the net widely and not get tied into just one potential relationship before the gathering ends. The important thing here is to exchange business cards. If you can get some additional info like a Facebook address then that would be an added bonus. Always make sure that you have a ready supply of your own cards to give away on these occasions. If you get a few moments to jot some notes on the back of the card you are given that would be excellent though that is seldom possible on these occasions. Memorize as much information as possible and jot it down as soon as possible. Having a few details with the card you have battled so hard to get makes it a much more valuable prize when you next use it. Once you have exchanged cards and made tentative agreements about meeting soon then make a polite get away and start the process with another person or group. By the time you finally get to leave you will hopefully have a bunch of new cards and the start of a business network that will be invaluable.

The little pile of business cards you have acquired is of little relevance unless you act upon them. Don't assume that just because you gave away a pile of your cards you have now set the ball in motion for a network to grow. It is possible that your cards will be filed away in a card file with dozens of others and never seen again. Your treasure trove lies in the card you collected not the cards you gave away. It is important that you act on those cards within twenty four to forty eight hours while you are still fresh in the minds of those you met with. Like you they will have met with many people during the course of the last few days and you need to transform yourself from just another face in the crowd into someone that will be remembered.

A good first move is to transcribe all the short hand notes you jotted down on the cards into a broader format. Some of the information you gleaned will not have been written down and now is the time to store it while you can still remember which bits of information went with which cards. These days there are many formats for storing this information but I still like to write mine down in good old not form logging the date of meeting, where it took place and any further relevant intelligence I might have gathered. Once I have all that information logged I can go through it and prioritize anything that needs to be acted on before the rest. For example, I may have heard the Bob's wife was having an operation today. I could drop him a quick e mail along the lines of "Hi Bob. My name is .... and we met at the function last night. You mentioned that your wife is having an operation today and I just wanted to say that I hope it all goes well." It sounds like a small thing but it places you in Bob's mind for a second time and demonstrates that you paid attention to what he had to say. Obviously this is just an example but I hope it shows how the network has started to develop and what value small seemingly unimportant pieces of information can be valuable.

In many cases you will not have gained such a useful handle but you can still send a follow up email stating how glad you were to have met the night before and mentioning that you hope to get together again soon. If there was an obvious opening to further meetings then you can ask for an appointment immediately but if things were less clear then content yourself with just a quick note designed to establish yourself in that other person's memory. This is a judgement call that only you can make relative to your unique circumstances but do be careful about coming on too strong even if you are eager to progress the relationship. Most relationships take time to mature and rushing forward may make you appear either too pushy of desperate. Often the person you have targeted to build into your network is more established than you are and he may be a little less keen to move things forward. Take your time and move cautiously. The door has to be opened rather than knocked down.

Chapter 5: The Second Meeting

If you are lucky you will have established that there is some sort of synergy right from the start and you are able to set up a meeting on that first follow up call. If not use the follow up call to establish yourself in their memory and then a few days later try to set up that vital second meeting. In many ways the second meeting uses similar techniques to the first but now the ice has been broken and you can be a little more proactive about presenting yourself. You still need to ask questions and use your active listening skills but now you can participate more in the conversation though it is always best to allow the other party to do most of the talking. A one third talking to two thirds listening ration seems to work quite well. You should differentiate between network building and marketing meetings. Even if selling a product or selling yourself is your long term aim, building that vital network should still be the priority and all too often we derail this with our desire to rush to the end goal without laying the necessary groundwork. In the short term you may be able to push forward and elicit a sale but with a longer term approach you could develop a relationship that opens the door to many sales.

Continue to look for handles to use at a later date. Look for areas of need that the other person has and then see if you can fill them in some way. For example, during the meeting he may mention that he is looking for a certain piece of equipment. If in a few days time you are able to locate something that his needs it gives you an excuse to make contact yet again. Better still it now creates a degree of indebtedness. Studies have revealed that people do not like to be indebted and so they are inclined to do something in return to eliminate that feeling. This is known as reciprocity and at first it may sound quite mercenary but what you are doing is looking for a need, filling that need and then having someone reciprocate by filling a need you may have.

Networking is an ongoing process and you need to constantly bear in mind that you must keep developing and fostering relationship in order to build on it. Your second meeting will hopefully lead to a third and so on. If things develop the way they should you will find yourself being invited into new circles that may not have been available to you before or which you may not even have considered. The overlap between one circle and the next does not really matter even if it is small. As you develop different circles so you will have contacts that may be of use in different ways. To go back to the last example and the piece of equipment you needed to find. Perhaps you knew someone in a completely different circle and thus were able to locate a source for the equipment needed. By tapping into contacts from the one circle you are able to use that to open a completely different circle.

Finally, don't be possessive of your contacts. Some people are mean spirited with contacts and hope that hiding one from the other they will benefit by being the middle man. In fact, the opposite is nearer the truth. If you have two contacts and you know that one could benefit from meeting the other then offer to put them together. Once again that simple piece of generosity that cost you nothing will engender reciprocity and may lead to your being paid back with interest.

Chapter 6: Social Media and Blogging

Twenty years ago the need to discuss social media in the field of networking would have been unnecessary. Today it is hardly possible to bring up the one subject without incorporating the other. Social media has become the go to tool for everyone from company executives to pop starts. Even politicians all now have web sites and twitter accounts. As a tool they can be highly effective at bringing us into contact with people we might want to connect with. The problem is, many people have begun to use these tools exclusively and I prefer to treat them as tools that enhance networking skills rather than tools that replace them. I have deliberately placed them further into the text of this book because I think that they are not as important or as useful as face to face meetings and they still require a certain amount of tact and diplomacy in their use. Many of the skills we have already dealt with are translatable, either directly or indirectly, to the social media field.

There are of course dozens, if not more, different platforms that can be used for networking. I will be dealing with the three main ones which are

Twitter, Facebook and LinkedIn. Right up front it is important to emphasize that if you are networking for the purposes of business then you need to stick to business in that area of whichever platform, or platforms, you choose to use. If you have a Facebook account that you use to contact family and friends and for sharing your latest batch of photographs then keep it to family and friends and don't bring your business associations into it. Your networking clients do not need to see the pics of your dog eating a watermelon and you certainly don't want them seeing you with too many beers down your neck dressed in your wife's bathrobe with a shower cap on your head. If you have an account of this type then keep it private though I would go one step further and warn you always to be very discerning about anything you put on the internet no matter what capacity it is in. (Clearly most of the world disagree with me on this particular subject)

The platform of preference for most business dealings seems to be LinkedIn. Although both Twitter and Facebook offer great possibilities in the business arena, LinkedIn is the main place that business type networking takes place. For that reason, I will start with LinkedIn and then take a shorter look at the other two. As I mentioned there are also many others which can still be very effective but they tend to be more specific to certain professions or groups of user.

LinkedIn

There are many books and sites that will give in depth information on the different ways to use this platform but I will deal with some general points that are most important. The first thing you have to consider is your personal profile and that may not be as easy as it appears. You really want to sit down and think what I am I trying to portray here and what are the most unique and positive aspects about me that will best serve that image. Are you selling yourself and your personal skills or are you presenting a product or service? I believe that what you are presenting first and foremost is your own character. Anything else that you are offering is secondary to who you are and the qualities that you offer. You are not Bob Smith, purveyor of fine pumps that have been manufactured for the last one hundred and fifty years and that come with a lifetime guarantee. You are Bob Smith, qualified and reliable marketing person with years of experience in the sales industry and a deep appreciation of customer needs. Oh and by the way at the moment you are selling these fine pumps. Networking, whether face to face or on social media platforms, is about who you are. People are not looking to build a relationship with a product; they are building a relationship with you. You are the networker.

The first few lines of your profile are the most crucial. All the rest, including qualifications and experience are very important but it is those first one or two sentences that may be your only chance of standing out from the crowd. I suggest you write out a profile and then sleep on it for the night and check it again in the morning before you post it.

Once you have a profile up and running you need to think about who you are going to attempt to link to and how you are going to go about that. Here is where you go back to your notes collected from the networking functions and you then filter out any that you may not feel would work for you on this particular platform. Once you have a selected target group it is time to search the platform and see if they are listed and then put in a connection request. Don't just send out a generic note saying Hi I would like to add you to my connections. You have some personal details you can include in your invitation and you may need to remind the person where you met and anything else that seems pertinent to connecting with them.

Fairly quickly and painlessly you will start to grow your network. You will also find that people will start to approach you to link up to their network. There are two differing schools of thought here. One is that you should have as many connections as possible and the other that you should keep your connections to people you have a definite affiliation with. The first school of thought is based on the principal that if you have thousands of connections you have a greater possibility of finding some sort of common interest with them. The second is that you can have a more in depth relationship with fewer key players and that those with thousands of connections are unable to follow them closely anyway. There is no right or wrong answer here. For some people the numbers game may play more in their favor whilst for others a tighter more targeted approach may be most beneficial. That will be best decided by you in terms of your own goals and objectives.

Whichever route you choose the rules are the same. Pay attention to what others have to say and make sure that whatever you say has value and is interesting. When your comments pop up on the screen you want people to feel that they must take a second look.

In networking terms, the big plus of LinkedIn is that is gives you a look at your connections contacts and there may well be people there that you want to reach out to. The best route is to go via your connection and give a brief explanation as to what mutual benefit there would be to his contact and yourself if he were to introduce you. People don't like to make introductions if their contact is then going to be bombarded with marketing pitches. If you present a logical and reasonable case for the introduction to be made then you overcome this resistance and the connection being approached will be much more willing to establish contact. As always in the network building game the way to move forward is slowly and gently.

One of the great upsides to LinkedIn is its groups and if you are building a network and want to establish your credibility this is the place to be. Groups enables you to target special interest areas that are pertinent to you. By following the various discussions you will get to know who the main players are and what their feeling is on certain subjects. Watch for a while and then start to participate and give positive feedback and input to their articles. Eventually you may have made enough of an impression to connect with them. At the very least you will have some insight into the way they think and what they are up to.

This is also the area where you will be able to post your own comments and start to be seen as a player in the field. You have some time here so make sure any comments are well thought out and researched and that you can back up what you have to say. Soon you will start to develop a following of your own and in general the groups tend to be like minded people who are quite supportive. There will, however, be those who are contrary often for no other reason than that they can be. The internet provides a voice for some who just want to be seen to have an opinion that is different. I suspect many of these mean spirited folk are the same sort that would not say boo to a mouse in the face to face world but now they can enter the fray from the shelter of their living room and give vent to their opinions. Be very careful how you deal with these situations. Present you argument clearly and politely and then step back. Often others following the discussion will step in and engage on your behalf. Your position now becomes one of observer. In depth social media rows will not help build your network.

Twitter

With just one hundred and forty characters to build a following, Twitter took some time to get my head around at first but has gone on to be my most useful social media tool. The one thing about this platform is that you soon learn that the world is packed full of people who want to say something even when they have nothing to say. I have not gone down the route of having thousands of followers just so I can say that I have them. I have tried to be really selective about who I follow yet still my time line is often littered with people who make the mistake of thinking that I really care what they had for breakfast. Twitter is excellent for gathering information fast. If you are following experts on certain subjects you very quickly see what they want to say and click to the articles that they normally attach to their tweets. It does not take long to work out who the movers and shakers are in your field and separate them from those that simply generate white noise. You have the option of creating lists and you can then put the people who really interest you in to those categories you have created. This enables you to make very quick assessments of what is happening at any given time on a given subject.

There is a certain etiquette to using Twitter which many people don't seem to grasp but which still remains important to the network builder. For starters this is not a communication tool like SMS. Twitter offers a perfectly effective direct message system to contact a person privately so there is no need to share with all you followers that you will be arriving at the restaurant in fifteen minutes and could the person you are meeting please order you a Martini. It is also important to be selective in what you tweet and only tweet material that is genuinely interesting to a large audience. If someone hogs the time line with a series of inane tweets, I immediately mute them. The ultimate compliment is to retweet somebody else's tweet but just as with your own tweets don't retweet inane comments purely in the hope of being followed by someone you would like to be connected to. Be considerate to all those followers and retweet material that is interesting and informative. You are trying to establish your own credentials so though you may be generous in retweeting bare in mind that people are following you because they want to know what you have to say so make sure you put up some interesting material of your own.

Twitter is a platform that really draws the trolls out of the woodwork. These nasty little people, for whom the word troll is ideally suited, love to attack people with contrary opinions. As with Facebook, the best way to deal with them is to step away and not engage which only feeds their frenzied minds. I prefer not to use this platform as a place to air really controversial views. Controversy does not work for me but for others it may be a tool that works in their favor though they need to be fairly brave.

Whilst there is no doubt that this platform has great potential to increase the size of your network I would like to end with one word of warning. Twitter along with all the other social networking platforms can be quite addictive and demanding of your time. It is easy to get carried away with reading tweets and creating tweets of your own but always ask yourself if what you are doing is being really constructive or if it is simply absorbing time that might be better used elsewhere.

Facebook

I have left the big daddy of social media platforms until last. I suspect that most people are now aware of this platform and how it works because it is so widely used on a private basis. Even if you have been using Facebook for yours to communicate with friends and family you need to remember that using it for network building is going to be totally different. Because you should not be muddling your network building affairs and your more personal life you will probably need to open a new page specific to the network you are building. Not only will you need to be careful what you put up on that page, you will also need to be circumspect as to who you invite into your circle because if somebody posts material that is not suitable to your image in some way or other you risk being associated with whatever it is they put up.

All the warnings aside this is still a great network building platform. Like the other two mentioned there are some rules you need to follow. You should be updating at least once or twice a day if you want to develop and maintain a high profile. Research shows that less than one third of Facebook users log in every day and another third once or twice per week. Consistency will therefore make you more noticeable.

Create content that encourages people to engage with you. Just like in the face to face meetings, start asking questions if you want to develop a conversation. Also when you are left a question make sure you reply. As with Twitter joining a few groups that are relevant to what you are trying to achieve and once you have observed for a while dive in and participate. You will soon discover that participating in group conversations regularly soon elevates your profile. Be careful not to over comment and always be polite and tolerant of others.

There are differing times when sites are most active and so by observing these you can start to be tactical about when you post your comments. Most people tend to be active of Facebook in the afternoon and then there is another rush in the evenings which is often occurring on portable devices. This will vary if for example you are approaching the platform from the East to the West coast of the US or the US from Europe. That may all seem a bit confusing at first but you will soon get the hang of it simply but watching when other posts are put up.

To increase your network you will need to be constantly inviting new contacts into your circle. Facebook has great tools for finding contacts and the groups themselves are a wonderful method of reaching people you have already qualified as being interested in   similar topics to those you are interested in.

One thing about both Facebook and Linked in is that they provide great reminders of things such as birthdays and change in working circumstances that become handles to say a quick hello.

All three of these platforms are so socially acceptable nowadays that they have transformed how we network. Interestingly though, the rules that were first developed in the face to face relationship area remain exactly the same only now you are able to network on a far larger scale. Those basics of common courtesy are still very applicable even if some choose not to use them. Listening to others and giving in order to get are intrinsic to any relationship building exercise.

To blog or not to blog

The choice to start you own blog or not is one you should consider carefully. I don't intend to tell you how to blog but we can take a brief look at some of the pros and cons in relation to your networking objectives.

Starting a blog definitely went through some fundamental changes in the last decade or so and it is now so easy that the average school kid can put one together. To make your blog stand out from the crowd and give a generally professional image may be a little more complicated and the time this entails will need to be weighed up. Of course if you have the money it need not be too very expensive to get a professional to build a site to your specifications. Whether you build it yourself or you hire in outside help make sure that the final product portrays you as competent.

Once you have your web site built you are ready to start providing content. The beauty about this is instead of now being reliant on other people to discuss the subjects that interest you or portray your project well, you can do this yourself. Once you publish you can link it through to your other social platforms or putting it up in the various groups you have joined. Not only do you control and create your own material you also have the option of using the tool as a handle in itself. For example, you can approach an expert in your field and ask if he would mind writing a guest blog or doing an interview. In networking terms this may be a tool too great not to use.

There are some down sides though. You have your blog up and running, you are writing content and developing a following and most importantly you are now master of your own destiny as far as material is concerned. The problem is that maintaining a blog is time consuming. You need to think of fresh content at least once a week and then you need to be a good enough wordsmith to put it together and technical enough to put in some photos or other media. After that if you start to gain traction you will start gathering followers who will leave comments and those will require replies. You may think you have miles of material to create some interesting posts, but do you have enough to do so week after week as well as run the rest of what goes to making up your life?

Overall if you are sure you can put together a blog and keep on top of all that running it well entails then I would say go for it. It certainly gives you much more freedom in generating content and if you can make it interesting you will gather followers and boost your network. I suggest writing out a fairly comprehensive list of content and providing you are sure you have enough articles buzzing around in your head to put together at least enough for a new weekly post every week for the first month or two then this is a powerful medium. Research the whole blogging subject well before you start and make sure you only put it out there if you can do it justice and it can do the same for you.

Conclusion

In essence, networking is about building relationships. Whether you want to do this from a business point of view or simply to expand your social life the skills required are the same. Social media platforms may have changed how we present this but don't be fooled; traditional values, manners and kindness are as valuable on dating sites, business network platforms or straight face to face meetings as they ever were. Much of what you have read here should be almost instinctive. The sort of thing your mother drummed into your head when you were a kid. Sadly, we live in a world where so much of this basic stuff has just been forgotten or pushed aside in the day to day rat race we call life.

Paying attention to other people, listening to them and showing interest in what makes them tick and offering help when you can provide it are not just networking skills. These are just the threads woven into the fabric of being a decent human being. The tools may have changed and evolved. The principals are timeless.

Made in the USA
Columbia, SC
23 June 2020

11894251R00028